TOM JACKSON   NICK SHEPHERD

FOLLOW THE LINK

A JOURNEY THROUGH TRANSPORTATION

FROM HOT LAVA TO A SPY ROCKET...

Quarto is the authority on a wide range of topics.

Quarto educates, entertains and enriches the lives of
our readers—enthusiasts and lovers of hands-on living.

www.quartoknows.com

Author: Tom Jackson
Illustrator: Nick Shepherd
Editors: Nancy Dickmann and Emily Pither
Designer: Adrian Morris

Copyright © QEB Publishing, Inc. 2017

First published in the United States
by QEB Publishing, Inc.
Part of The Quarto Group
6 Orchard
Lake Forest, CA 92630

A CIP record for this book is available from the Library of Congress.

ISBN 978 1 60992 956 5

Printed in China

FSC
www.fsc.org
MIX
Paper from
responsible sources
FSC® C104723

CONTENTS

INTRODUCTION...4

BURNING ROCKS...6

IN A CAVE...8

DARK GLASS...10

MAKING METALS...12

ACCIDENTAL DISCOVERIES...14

BRONZE AGE LEGENDS...16

WHIRLS TO WHEELS...18

HIGH-SPEED TRAVEL...20

THE RISE OF IRON...22

DISCOVERING MAGNETS...24

COMPASSES...26

HENRY THE NAVIGATOR...28

THE VOYAGE OF COLUMBUS...30

DEAD RECKONING...32

LATITUDE...34

LONGITUDE...36

COPPER BOTTOMS...38

MASS PRODUCTION...40

STEAM POWER...42

TAKING TO THE AIR...44

IRONCLADS AND STEAM LINERS...46

GOING LOCO...48

INNER FIRE...50

DREADNOUGHTS...52

HITTING THE TARGET...54

JET ENGINES...56

ROTOR BLADES...58

STEALTH IN THE SKIES...60

SPY SATELLITES...62

GPS NAVIGATION...64

THE SPACE SHUTTLE...66

TOUGH TILES...68

SUPER-JUMBO VEHICLES...70

SPY ROCKETS...72

AN ELEVATOR TO SPACE...74

TIMELINE...76

GLOSSARY...78

INDEX...80

INTRODUCTION

There is a robot spaceplane flying around the Earth right now—we think. It is top secret, and with no human crew on board it can stay in space for months or years at a time. This spy rocket is tough enough to travel in and out of space many times over. To find out how, we need to trace it back to the beginning.

ROCKS AND CRYSTALS

The plane is only possible because ancient people once got a surprise when they put some rocks in a fire. It can find its own way through space because Christopher Columbus thought the world was three times too small, and its rocket engine originally comes from yellow crystals that melt into blood—or at least that's what it looks like! How does any of this make sense? To find out, you have to follow the link.

NEW DISCOVERIES

What we know about the world keeps changing. What we know now is different from what people knew in the past, and in the future we will discover new ways of understanding how it all works. Discoveries do not come out of nowhere, though. Smart people figure out new things from what they know already—and they often get their ideas from very strange places.

THE BIRTH OF TRANSPORTATION

This book tells the story of how we figured out how to unlock the materials found in nature, then put them to work to transport us wherever we want to go. Cold rocks were turned into hot metals, invisible forces were picked up by carved stones, and sand and soot were used to make the toughest spacecraft ever.

I DIDN'T KNOW THAT!

Along the way, we will learn that Hercules nearly got killed by bad breath, weathercasters used to study meteors, and miners were once very afraid of gnomes. You'll even discover why Chinese architects make holes in their buildings (it's for the dragons, obviously).

The story starts at the crater of a volcano, still smoldering after an eruption. Where will it take us? Let's follow the link.

BURNING ROCKS

A volcano can be a very colorful place. As well as hot orange—red lava, you may also find rainbow pools of simmering water, gooey brown mud that burps out stinky gases, and lumps of crusty yellow crystals scattered across the ground.

BLOOD FROM A STONE

The yellow crystals are sulfur. This element is one of the few that is found pure in nature, and the best place to find it is around volcanoes. The pure sulfur can burn very hot, melting into a thick red liquid that looks like blood.

BLUE LAVA

Occasionally volcanos erupt liquid sulfur. It catches on fire in the air, making streams of blue lava instead of the normal red stuff.

HELLFIRE

Ancient people called sulfur *brimstone*, which means "burning rock." They thought brimstone came from the underworld, a terrible place filled with fires, where demons and devils tormented the ghosts of evil people after they had died.

THE GATES OF HELL

Sulfur burns in air to make a poisonous gas. Volcanoes make other deadly gases that are heavier than air, and these gases fill deep caves. Ancient explorers who ventured into these caves often never came out—and the caves became known as the gates of hell.

BAD BREATH

Hercules, the hero from Roman legends, was sent to battle the Hydra. This horrible beast lived in a cave, and it could kill you with a blast of its terrible breath.

EXPLODING POWDER

Powdered sulfur is one of the ingredients in gunpowder. It is mixed with charcoal and saltpeter, and together these chemicals can burn so fast that they explode all at once.

WHAT'S NEXT?

Luckily, not all caves are so deadly. Many provided our ancestors with a safe place to live.

IN A CAVE

We sometimes call our distant ancestors "cavemen" even though most of them did not live underground at all. However, caves are quiet, hidden places, and that makes them a good place to set up a safe home. For the same reason, they are easily forgotten about. There are many caves where no one has set foot for thousands of years.

HIDDEN HOMES

The skeletons and stone tools of prehistoric humans have been found in caves all over the world. Some of these ancient finds have been hidden away, safe from the weather—and later humans—for more than two million years. However, a cave that was inhabited about 35,000 years ago in Sulawesi, Indonesia, had something else: a cave painting.

MATHEMATICAL BONE

We call the earliest period of human history the Stone Age because most of what is left from that time are stone tools. However, Stone Age people also used wood, shells, and bones. The Ishango Bone, carved in central Africa 20,000 years ago, is covered in sets of tally marks showing different numbers. The bone is believed to be the world's oldest calculator.

MAKING PICTURES

Around this time, humans began painting their caves. They made pictures of animals, such as cows and deer, and strange mythical creatures. They drew dark lines with charcoal, which is wood that has burned very slowly until it becomes soft and black.

GONE BUT NOT FORGOTTEN

Some cave paintings in Australia may show animals that are now extinct, including huge flightless birds and giant wombats.

SQUIRT SILHOUETTE

Early cave paintings contain handprints. They were made by the artist placing their hand on the rock and spraying it with paint from their mouth.

COLORED CHEMICALS

More colorful paints were made from powdered metal-rich rocks mixed with water. To make brown paint, early people used umber, a mixture of iron, aluminum, and manganese oxides. To make white, they used calcite, a form of calcium carbonate. Red was from red ocher (dried iron oxide) and yellow was from yellow ocher (a chemical called iron hydroxide).

WHAT'S NEXT?

To paint a self-portrait, a cave artist would need a mirror. The oldest known mirrors were polished pieces of volcanic glass, a material that had other uses too.

DARK GLASS

Volcanic glass is called obsidian. This smooth, shiny rock was very useful in ancient times. As well as being used to make the first mirrors, the dark, natural glass was made into super-sharp cutting tools and weapons. Even today, the very sharpest blades used by surgeons are made from obsidian, not metal.

COOL IT!

Obsidian is very dark and not see-through. This is because it contains tiny pieces of minerals. It is made when lava cools down so fast that it doesn't have time to form crystals. Instead, the sand-like minerals in the lava solidify into a tangled jumble, which makes it smooth and hard—but also easily cracked and smashed.

YIKES!

FLOATING ROCKS

When lava that is filled with gas bubbles erupts from volcanoes under the sea, it cools quickly into a soft rock called pumice. The bubbles are trapped inside the solid rock, so the lumps of pumice float to the surface. They can form huge "rafts" dozens of miles long.

LAVA BOMBS

Blobs of molten rock thrown out of volcanoes above ground begin to cool as they fly through the air. As they travel, they form into a long, bullet-like shape. By the time they land, the lava has become a solid stone missile, known as a lava bomb. Take cover!

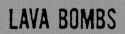

SHARP STONES

Stone Age tools were made by a process called knapping. A rock, such as a flint, was knocked against a larger and harder one. Each knock chipped the flint, leaving a sharp edge that could be used for cutting and slicing.

GLASS SWORDS

Obsidian could also be knapped to give it sharp edges. The oldest obsidian cutting tool is more than 1.5 million years old. Obsidian tools were especially common in ancient America. Mayan soldiers, from what is now Mexico and Guatemala, used a terrifying weapon called a *macuahuitl*. This was a stick covered in razor-sharp obsidian blades to make a weapon that was half-sword, half-ax.

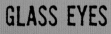

GLASS EYES

Easter Island is famous for the huge statues that cover the hillside. These statues originally had carved eyes, and the dark pupils were made from obsidian.

WHAT'S NEXT?

Obsidian is very sharp, but it is also brittle and breaks when dropped. About 10,000 years ago, a new material was discovered. It was tougher, and it changed the world.

MAKING METALS

About 8,000 years ago in what is now Turkey, someone saw a liquid trickling from a fire. It flickered red—hot and was gooey like molasses. Even stranger, when it cooled down, it formed a smooth solid. What was this mysterious substance?

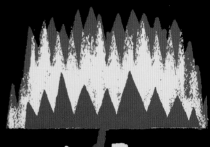

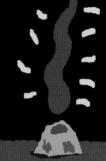

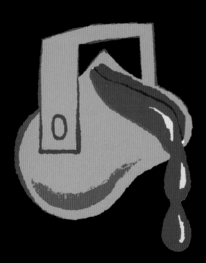

SMELTING

However, the lead oozing from the fire was different—it had come out of a rock, like magic. Lead-rich minerals in the rock reacted with the carbon in the burning wood. The carbon took the place of the lead in the mineral, leaving behind pure metal. This process is now known as smelting.

USING LEAD

Lead is a heavy, gray metal that is easy to bend and hammer flat. It was too soft to make blades sharper than flints, and it wasn't beautiful like gold. In ancient times, it was used to make necklace beads and ammunition for slings. We now know that it is poisonous, so we do not use it much today.

Lead was used in jewelry as well as makeup. It was dangerous but desirable!

MAGICAL METALS

Our unknown fire watcher had found a metal called lead. At that time, metals were not entirely unknown. Copper, silver, and gold were occasionally found pure in rocks, and meteorites made of pure iron were the most valuable of all.

SPACE ROCKS

Meteorites are space rocks that have crashed into Earth. Most rocks like this burn up in the air, and only a few get all the way to the ground. They explode on impact and there is seldom much left. The largest lump of left-over meteorite ever found is only about 9 feet (2.7 meters) wide!

SPACE WEATHER?

Until the 19th century, people thought meteors were caused by the weather, not space rocks. That is why the study of the weather is called meteorology.

NATURALLY PURE

Gold was probably the first metal ever used by humans. Ancient people spotted glittering nuggets in riverbeds and made precious objects with them. Gold does not react with air or water, so a gold crown, coin, or ring will never rust away. It will stay shiny—and fabulous—forever!

WHAT'S NEXT?

People may have discovered smelting while they were firing clay pottery in a kiln. The stones used to build a kiln could have been smelted by accident. And the accidental discoveries did not end there...

ACCIDENTAL DISCOVERIES

Over the centuries, people learned which rocks made good ores, or sources of metal. The best ores seemed to be dark and shiny rocks. By chance, they found new kinds of materials, and discovered better ways of making them.

BRIGHTER, BETTER?

The dark lead ores often also contained silver, which was used in jewelry.

Sometimes the metal coming from the ores was lighter and whiter. This was known as "bright lead," but we now know it as tin. Both tin and lead were soft enough to bend and hammer flat, so they were used to make into pipes.

WATER WORKERS

The Latin word for lead was *plumbum*, and scientists still use the symbol Pb for this metal. People who work with water pipes are also called plumbers, because their ancient co-workers used lead.

PLUMBERS R US

GETTING HOTTER

About 7,000 years ago in the Balkans, people found an entirely new metal. This one came from ores that were green and blue. Smelting these ores produced a reddish metal, which we now call copper. Copper is much harder than lead or tin, and can be made sharper. The Copper Age had begun.

ICE AND FIRE

In ancient Iraq, they used the same word for ice and copper ore. Both were rare and valuable, and they both did the same thing: they turned into liquid when they got hotter.

I ASKED FOR ICE!

WAX CASTS

Early coppersmiths also kept bees. They used beeswax to make molds to cast their metal. They made a model of the shape they wanted out of wax, then put clay around it. The beeswax was then melted and poured out—and the hot metal was poured in.

USEFUL WASTE

To smelt copper, people needed super-hot, charcoal-fueled furnaces. Among the ash left behind, they found glass. It was hard and brittle, but light could shine through it. It was thousands of years before people learned how to make usable glass. Around 3000 BCE in Egypt and Mesopotamia, people learned to heat sand-like minerals. The crystals melted into a soft goo that could be shaped while still hot, before cooling solid.

WHAT'S NEXT?

Ancient craftspeople now had a range of new materials to work with. However, the next big step came when they started mixing them together.

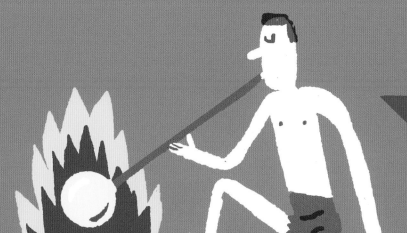

BRONZE AGE LEGENDS

Around 5,000 years ago, the Copper Age turned into the Bronze Age. Adding tin and other minerals to copper makes bronze, a metal alloy that is tougher and longer–lasting than pure copper.

CIVILIZATION BEGINS

The Bronze Age began on the eastern shores of the Mediterranean Sea, where powerful kings ruled over large cities. Their tough armies had bronze weapons that could slice through the copper armor of their enemies. It was a time of great empires, legends, and heroes.

FLOOD STORIES

Many cultures have legends about a great flood—Noah's ark is just one of them. Another version, from 4,700 years ago, is about Gilgamesh, a king in a region known as Mesopotamia. The Tigris and Euphrates rivers, which run through the area, made the land good for farming. A plentiful food supply let cities grow large, so many Bronze Age civilizations appeared here.

GREEK LEGENDS

The Minoans were a Bronze Age civilization on the Greek island of Crete. Their ruler, King Minos, was rumored to be protected by a half-bull, half-man monster called the Minotaur who lived in a maze called the Labyrinth. Theseus, a hero from the Greek mainland, finally killed the Minotaur.

THE TROJAN WAR

About 3,200 years ago, more Greeks from the mainland attacked Troy, a city on the coast of what is now Turkey. The Greek writer Homer wrote about the exploits of famous soldiers such as Achilles and Odysseus and the wooden horse used by the invaders to finally defeat the Trojans.

WHAT'S NEXT?

Tough Bronze Age weapons changed the world forever, but a much more important invention was about to be made—and it all began because people wanted prettier pots.

LOST CITY

Some people think that the legend of Atlantis, a great city that sank into the sea, was actually about the Minoans. About 3,500 years ago, a volcanic island near Greece exploded. A Minoan city on the island fell into the sea, and a tsunami destroyed the Minoan navy—leaving them defenseless.

WHIRLS TO WHEELS

Metalworkers were important people in Bronze Age society. However, it was the technology used by potters, farmers, and construction workers that led to today's machines.

IN A SPIN

Early potters made bowls by looping a long string of clay into a coil, then smoothing it all together. But one day, someone in Sumeria realized that if the board they put the coil on could spin around, it would make it easier. They invented a round board that could spin by itself. Sounds a lot like a wheel, doesn't it? Today's potters still use wheels to shape wet clay with their fingers.

THE PULLEY

Water from wells is raised using a windlass, a wheel turned by a handle so that a rope winds around it. A bucket at the other end of the rope can be raised or lowered by turning the wheel. Connecting more wheels makes it easier to lift heavier weights —becoming a very useful machine called a pulley.

HEAVY LIFTER

Ancient Egyptians made use of another simple machine to build the pyramids. A ramp makes it easier to lift heavy things, like a slab of stone. The slab is raised with many small shoves instead of one big heave. Stairs are ramps built for feet!

BONE CHINA

Natural clay is heavy, but around 2,000 years ago, a lightweight version was developed in China. The ash from burned bones was added to the clay, making "bone china." It was strong but much easier to handle.

MACHINE AGE

Another Bronze Age machine was the *shaduf*, a long lever for lifting water to use on crops. All levers have a turning point called a fulcrum. Moving one side makes the other side move in the opposite direction. By shifting the position of the fulcrum, you can adjust the speed and power of the lever.

CRACKING JOB

Egyptian pyramid builders could not cut stone, even with bronze tools. So they used another machine—wedges made from wood. The wedge was hammered into a small crack and then soaked in water. The wet wood expanded, cracking the rock.

WHAT'S NEXT?

We still use these machines today, in different ways. The free-spinning wheel may have been invented by Sumerian potters, but it did not take long for it to be used in vehicles.

HIGH-SPEED TRAVEL

All through the Bronze Age, people had put strong animals, such as oxen, camels, and even elephants, to work carrying heavy loads. The animals sometimes hauled cargo in boxy sleds. But then a picture from Sumeria, made around 4,500 years ago, showed something new.

CART CRAZY

The Sumerian picture showed a sled with four solid wood wheels on it. Let's call it a cart. Carts quickly became the fastest thing on wheels— because they were the *only* thing on wheels! Sumerian carts were pulled by donkeys. Carts protected by a thick armor of animal skins could carry spear-throwers into battle. It would have been a rough, slow ride.

ROLLERS AND BALLS

The potter's wheel was probably the inspiration for adding wheels and axles to make the first carts. However, before this, loads were slid over cut logs that worked as rollers. The builders of Stonehenge in England may have used rollers to move their giant stones. Another theory is that they rolled the heavy slabs over stone balls running in wooden tracks.

WINNING TECHNOLOGY

Soon every army in the region was using these war carts. In 1650 BCE, Egypt was invaded by a group called the Hyksos, whose technology was far superior—they traveled in two-wheeled chariots. The chariot wheels had spokes, making them strong but lightweight, so they could be much bigger (and faster) than solid wood wheels. The chariots were pulled by teams of horses, which were unknown in Egypt. It took a century for the Egyptians to rebuild their army (with chariots!) and retake their land.

TRAVELING COACH CLASS

A coach is a cart with a bouncy suspension, which makes it more comfortable. This comfy design was invented in the Hungarian town of Koc (pronounced "Kotch") in the 15th century.

WHAT'S NEXT?

The technology used by the Hyksos was similar to that of the Hittite people from what is now Turkey. And the Hittites were about to make another amazing leap in technology.

HORSEPOWER

Power is a measure of how much work a machine is doing in every second. There are many ways to measure it, but the oldest is horsepower. A horse has the power of one horsepower, while a Formula 1 race car can produce 1,000 horsepower!

THE RISE OF IRON

Around the year 1200 BCE, the kingdoms of the Bronze Age, from Greece to Egypt, were in crisis. They had run out of a good supply of tin. Without it they could not make bronze, and without bronze they could not defend their lands. A new source of hard metal was needed.

IRONWORKING

The replacement metal was iron. Iron is much more common in rocks than tin or copper, but it requires a much hotter furnace to smelt it. No one knows where iron was first produced. Ancient ironworks have been found in western Syria, Turkey (home of the Hittites), and Bulgaria. The oldest of all—3,500 years old—are in Niger in Africa.

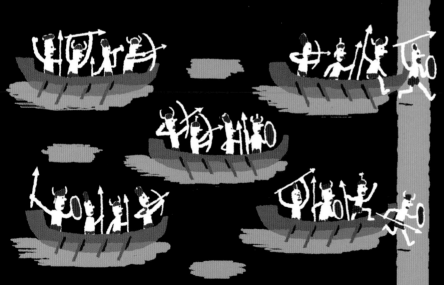

MYSTERY INVADERS

The change from the Bronze Age to the Iron Age is called the Bronze Age Collapse. Great civilizations such as the Hittites and Mycenaeans disappeared. At the same time, Egyptian history records waves of invaders who arrived in ships. The Egyptians called them the Sea Peoples, and we can only make guesses about who they were.

STEELY STUFF

It is likely that coppersmiths in many different places came across iron by accident when they made their furnaces extra hot. Pure iron (known as wrought iron) is fairly soft and bendy, but people learned to make what we now call steel. Steel is iron mixed with a small amount of carbon. It is the same weight as bronze, but much harder.

A NEW AGE

Iron and steelmaking technology spread. People in northern Europe started using iron in about 600 BCE, and it was used in Japan about 300 years later. By this time, new sources of tin had been found, but it was too late—iron now ruled the world.

DISCOVERING BRITAIN

Pytheas, an ancient Greek explorer, made the first written record of Britain in 325 BCE, and reported that its region of Belerion (now known as Cornwall) was a rich source of tin. He named the land Bretannike, which probably comes from the ancient Welsh word *prydein* (ancient Britons spoke Welsh). *Prydein* means "the people of shapes" and refers to the way Britons covered themselves in tattoos and paint. So Britain is the "land of the tattooed people."

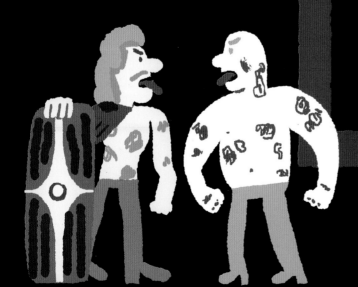

WHAT'S NEXT?

Iron objects were not only stronger than bronze, but also cheaper. And there was another thing that made iron a very special metal indeed…

DISCOVERING MAGNETS

The main iron ores used since the Iron Age are hematite and magnetite. Both are made of iron and oxygen, but they look rather different. Hematite is a red mineral—its name means "blood stone" in Greek—and it is one of the main chemicals in Stone Age paints. Magnetite, on the other hand, is shiny and black.

LAND OF LODESTONES

Magnetite is named after Magnesia, an ancient kingdom in what is now Turkey. Around 600 BCE, a Greek philosopher named Thales discovered that some lumps of this dark rock—known as lodestones—had a strange power. They could attract and repel each other, and iron things stuck to them. Thales had given us the first description of a magnet.

FOLLOWING YOUR NOSE

Birds, insects, shellfish, and even bacteria have tiny crystals of magnetite in their bodies. These work like tiny compasses, helping the animals find their way around. Birds, for example, have magnets in their upper beaks, so they really are following their noses when they fly.

RED PLANET

Iron ore is what makes the planet Mars look red—even without a telescope. Its blood-red color is why it was named after Mars, the Roman god of war. When the first probes landed on the planet in the 1970s, they found that the planet is covered in a layer of dust made from hematite. Hematite on Earth forms under water, so Mars may have once had a huge ocean like ours.

GEOMANCY

Lodestones were also investigated in China, and by 100 CE they were being used as "south governors." These lodestones were carved into spoon shapes. When placed on a flat surface, the south governor always pointed south. The ancient Chinese used their lodestone spoons to show the best places to build villages and temples.

FENG SHUI

The ancient Chinese practice of feng shui is based on the idea that there are good and bad spirits flowing through the landscape. These spirits could be upset by buildings in the wrong place. Chinese architects still follow the rules of feng shui. Many skyscrapers in China are built with "dragon holes," which are large gaps that allow spirits to move freely between the mountains and the sea—and they look good, too.

WHAT'S NEXT?

Modern versions of the south governor point north. It took nearly 1,000 years, but eventually lodestones were used as compasses for finding your way around.

25

COMPASSES

A compass always points in the same direction, so travelers can be sure which way they are heading. However, it took nearly a thousand years for people to begin using lodestone compasses for finding their way around.

FLOATING POINTER

A compass that worked on the move had to be designed to be tough. The first navigation compass was developed in China. The spoon-shaped pointer of the south governor was slimmed down to a simple lodestone needle. This floated in a bowl of water, where it was free to swing around.

COMPASS ROSE

The dry compass had a rose pattern inside, which showed the four main, or cardinal, directions: north, east, south, and west.

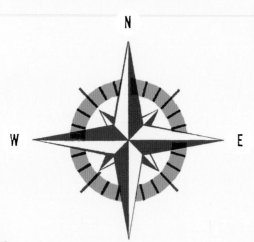

METAL FARMER

In 1556, Georgius Agricola, a German miner, wrote a book about metals, and explained how pure iron could be made into a magnet. All you had to do was line the iron up, north to south, and heat it gently while giving it little taps.

DRY COMPASS

By the 13th century, Arab and European travelers had learned about compasses. A new European dry compass design had a needle balanced on a pin inside a box. The dry compass was bolted to the center of a ship so it always showed where it was going.

WRONG WAY!

VIKING SUNSTONE

The Vikings didn't need a compass for long journeys. They could navigate by the Sun, even on a cloudy day. Some sources say they looked through a clear crystal, called a sunstone. This may have been calcite, which splits the light in two. Twisting the crystal so the light beams join together shows you where the sunlight is coming from.

WILLIAM GILBERT
1544–1603

IRON GLOBE

In 1600, William Gilbert carved a model Earth out of a lodestone. He used it to show that a compass works because it is being attracted to Earth, which is a giant magnet. A compass points to magnetic north. This point is about 750 miles (1,200 kilometers) from the true North Pole, but it moves around. At the moment it is heading north at about 25 miles (40 kilometers) per year.

WHAT'S NEXT?

The compass made long-distance navigation safer, and a prince whose kingdom was on the farthest edge of the world decided to use it to explore the unknown.

HENRY THE NAVIGATOR

Prince Henrique of Portugal is better known as Henry the Navigator.
In the 1400s, Portugal was the most western part of the known world.
Beyond it lay the Atlantic Ocean—and perhaps the edge of the world.

EXPLORERS WANTED

Portugal was at the western end
of the Silk Road, a long, overland
trading system that connected
Europe to India and China. Henry
realized that he could get to Asia by
using the sea instead. He ordered
a team of explorers to find new sea
routes to the east.

I NEED MORE SHIPS!

PRINCE HENRIQUE
1394–1460

NEW SHIPS NEEDED

Henry's explorers would need a fleet
of tough sailing ships. They had to
be small, fast, and easy to steer—
and able to sail long distances into
the unknown. For inspiration, his
shipbuilders looked at the designs
of ships from around the world.

TOP SHIPS

Viking longships were known for their tough, rounded hulls,
which could stay afloat in rough seas. Mediterranean galleys
were built for fighting, with ports (openings) on the side for
cannons to fire through. They also had fortress decks known
as the forecastle and aftcastle. The Chinese junk was the
first ship to use a rudder. As for sails, the Arab dhow used a
triangular, or lateen, sail that could sail toward the wind as
well as away from it.

PICK AND MIX

Henry's ship, the caravel, took the best points of each of these ships. It had a rudder and two masts with square and lateen sails. It was defended by cannon ports and had an aftcastle. The hull was like a longship but the wooden planks were fitted smoothly together so it could move faster.

LEFT AND RIGHT

Before rudders, a large oar called a steerboard was placed on the right side of a ship. At a port, the ship always docked with its left side against the quay. As a result, left and right on a ship are called "port" and "starboard."

WHAT'S NEXT?

Henry's explorers found new Atlantic islands and traveled all the way around Africa to reach India. Soon sailors from other countries joined in—and one in particular had a very bold idea.

THE VOYAGE OF COLUMBUS

Christopher Columbus, an Italian sea captain, is the most famous explorer of all time. In 1492, he decided to reach Asia by sailing west—and he discovered what he thought was India!

SO CRAZY, IT JUST MIGHT WORK

Columbus' idea was to sail all the way around the world, ending up in Asia. It is often said that everyone else back then thought the world was flat. In fact, people had known for many years that Earth was a sphere. Most people still thought it was a crazy plan, though. It took years to convince anyone to fund his voyage.

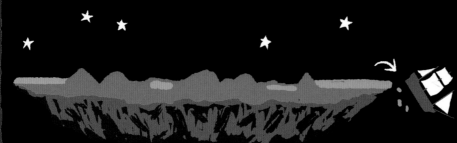

CHRISTOPHER COLUMBUS
1451–1506

ROUND WORLD

Three clues showed ancient people that Earth is a sphere. First, during an eclipse, the shadow of Earth on the Moon is always round. Second, when a ship travels over the horizon, the mast appears first, then the hull—as if it is sailing uphill. Last, the stars you can see change when you travel north or south. If the world was flat, you'd get the same view of the sky from everywhere.

SMALL WORLD?

Columbus thought the world was actually much smaller than people believed, and that he could sail around it in a few weeks. The experts warned that he'd got it wrong and would run out of water and food.

LAND AHOY!

After 33 days at sea, the crew spotted islands. Columbus described the people who lived there as Indians, thinking he was in East Asia. However, he was in the Caribbean, and the islands were part of an entirely different continent: America.

DIVIDING IT UP

In 1494, the Pope announced a dividing line in the middle of the ocean, about 1,000 miles (1,600 kilometers) west of Africa. Spain could have everything to the west, and Portugal got the east. Spain took over most of South America. However, Brazil stretched over Portugal's side of the line, so it went to them.

MEASURING THE WORLD

In 200 BCE, the Greek mathematician Eratosthenes calculated that the distance around the world was 24,900 miles (40,041 kilometers). He got it almost exactly right. However, Columbus thought the world was a third of this size.

WHAT'S NEXT?

Columbus calculated that he could travel fast enough to reach land before running out of supplies. Part of his calculation was done using a rope, a float, and some knots!

DEAD RECKONING

A compass told an explorer which direction the ship was heading in, but it could not say where it was, how far it had come, or how far it needed to go. For that, they used a system called dead reckoning.

NEED TO KNOW

A navigator using dead reckoning needed to know three things: direction, speed, and starting point. He could then plot the ship's position and guide it to its destination. The compass showed direction, but the other two factors were more difficult to figure out.

KNOTTED ROPE

Speed was calculated by throwing a wooden float behind the ship. As it floated away, the log pulled a rope with it. This rope was divided into equal lengths by knots, and the crew counted how many knots of rope were pulled out in half a minute. This gave them the ship's speed, and even today speeds at sea are measured in knots.

NAUTICAL MILE

Today, one knot is the same speed as one nautical mile per hour. A nautical mile is 1.15 miles (1.85 kilometers). It would take 900 days to sail all the way around the world at a speed of one knot.

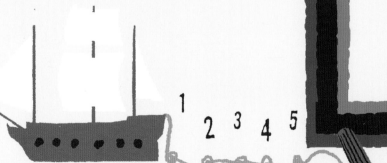

UPSIDE DOWN

The telescope was invented in 1608, making it easier to search for landmarks. However, in early designs, everything you saw was flipped upside down!

WIND DIRECTIONS

Winds swirl in loops—the ones in the northern hemisphere go clockwise and in the south they are counterclockwise. This is because Earth rotates from west to east, so the surface of the planet is always moving to the side as the winds blow over it.

WHAT'S NEXT?

Dead reckoning was very hit-and-miss, and ships often missed their destination. Luckily, there was another method for measuring a position while at sea, which used the Sun.

LANDMARKS

It was important for the navigator to know where the ship's course began. That was easy when they left port, but often a course would have to zigzag across the sea to catch the wind. Navigators would scan for landmarks, like islands or rocks, to help them get a "fix" on their position.

33

LATITUDE

Latitude is a measure of how far you are north or south of the equator. The idea is an ancient one, and navigators knew they could find their latitude by measuring the height of the Sun.

SEASONAL SHIFTS

In summer, the Sun rises higher above the horizon than in winter—which is why it gets so hot! The Sun is also higher when you look from the equator, and it gets lower in the sky as you go north or south. If you know the date, the Sun's height tells you how far you are from the equator.

TIME FOR LUNCH

TRICKY MEASUREMENT

The Sun is at its highest at noon each day, so this is the best time to measure its position. It is easy to do on land but much harder while standing on the rolling deck of a ship. An invention called the sextant solved that problem.

SHADOW CLOCK

A sundial tells the time using shadows. They are longest in the morning and evening, and shortest at noon. The Sun casts a shadow of a sundial's central post, or gnomon. The world's largest sundial is in Jaipur, India. Its gnomon is 92 feet (28 meters) high and it can measure time to an accuracy of 2 seconds.

GOING BY DEGREES

Latitude is measured in degrees, and there are 360 of them in a circle. This system was invented long ago by the Babylonians, who counted in 60s. They used 60 because it divided neatly into so many smaller numbers. Each degree is divided into 60 minutes, and each minute is divided into 60 seconds. We divide time in the same way.

TWO VIEWS

The sextant was developed in 1730 by John Hadley. It had a mirror eyepiece that showed the horizon and the Sun at the same time. A navigator would then line them up to get the angle of the Sun and calculate the latitude. Unfortunately, this only solved half the problem. Sailors also needed to know their longitude, or position east and west—and no one knew how to do that.

If you traveled one degree of latitude each hour, it would take 15 days to go around the world.

The sundial in Jaipur, India, was built in the 1730s.

WHAT'S NEXT?

In 1707, 1,550 sailors drowned when a fleet of British warships went off course and crashed into rocks. Figuring out how to measure longitude had suddenly become very urgent.

LONGITUDE

In 1714, the British government offered a huge cash prize to anyone who could calculate a ship's longitude during a voyage. People came up with all kinds of ideas, but the simplest one was to use a clock.

AND THE WINNER IS...

The main winner was a clockmaker named John Harrison. Back then, clocks were not very accurate and needed to be reset every day. Over nearly 30 years, Harrison built better clocks that always stayed accurate, even when tossed around in a ship.

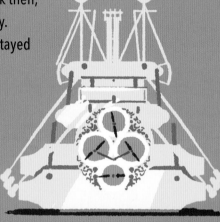

Harrison's first attempt had swinging parts to counteract the motion of the ship.

LOCAL NOON

But how can a clock show longitude? You probably know that the time is often different in other places. Noon is the time when the Sun is at its highest point in the sky. Earth constantly spins, making it look like the Sun moves through the sky. As a result, it is always noon somewhere on Earth.

BEFORE AND AFTER

At noon, the Sun is directly above a line of longitude running from the North Pole to the South Pole. This imaginary line is called a meridian. Morning times are called "a.m.," an abbreviation for "ante (before) meridian" and afternoon times are "p.m." for "post (after) meridian."

COMPARING TIMES

The Earth spins 360 degrees in 24 hours, so every hour it moves by 15 degrees. London, England, is at 0° longitude, while Prague is almost exactly 15° east. This means that noon (and lunch!) in Prague happens an hour before it does in London.

JOHN HARRISON
1693–1776

Harrison's third clock took him 19 years to
build, but it still wasn't accurate enough.

THERE'S NO TIME LIKE HOME

A ship's clock shows the time back at port. A navigator can use his sextant to measure noon where the ship is, then compare that time with the clock. The difference shows how far east or west the ship is. Harrison's clocks allowed ships to make longer voyages and stay away from port for months, or even years.

WHAT'S NEXT?

Despite all the latest navigation technology, old-fashioned wooden ships still faced many dangers—including attacks by worms!

TIME ZONES

Using noon to set a clock causes problems, because it makes the time slightly different in different parts of the country. Instead, most countries have a standard time that is correct everywhere. Large countries, like the United States, may have several time zones.

COPPER BOTTOMS

Thanks to their cutting-edge navigation technology, the British Royal Navy soon became the largest military force on the sea. Its ships sailed across the world, but when they got back to port many were badly damaged. The damage was not from battles, but tiny shipworms.

SHELLFISH IN WORM'S CLOTHING

Shipworms have wormlike bodies with two tiny shells on their heads, which scrape away wood. The shipworms eat the wood, and they see no difference between a dead log floating in the ocean and a state-of-the art warship.

SNAIL DYE

The fleet of the ancient Phoenicians was paid for by shellfish, not destroyed by it. About 3,000 years ago, Phoenician merchants traded a rare and expensive dye made from tiny sea snails. Only kings and emperors could afford it, and it became known as royal purple—although it was actually a deep red.

RED BUGS

In the 17th century, Spain's navy brought back cochineal, a red dye made from insects that lived in Mexico. Cochineal was much cheaper than royal purple, and for the first time ordinary Europeans could afford red clothes.

PROTECTIVE COATING

The tunnels made by shipworms did not show from the outside, but they weakened the timbers. A ship riddled with worms could collapse at any moment. Shipbuilders tried coating the hull with sulfur. That didn't work, and neither did using tar. Covering a ship in lead worked—but the ship nearly sank from the weight!

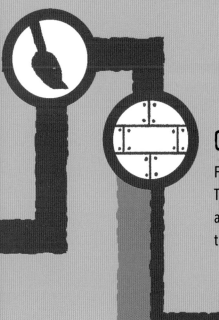

COPPER COATING

Finally, it was found that covering the bottom of a ship in copper solved the problem. The worms couldn't get to the wood, and the copper reacted with seawater to produce a slime that kept seaweed from growing on the hull. In 1770, the Royal Navy ordered that all their ships be copper-bottomed.

WHAT'S NEXT?

The British were constantly at war, so they had a lot of warships. Coppering them all would rely on a faster and more efficient way of making things: mass production.

RECIPE FOR SUCCESS

Using copper on ships was so successful that "copper-bottomed" became a term that meant "sure to succeed."

MASS PRODUCTION

In the 14th century, in Venice, Italy, mass production meant that 16,000 shipyard workers could build one new ship every day. Around 500 years later, British shipyards were also made more efficient, as part of what became the Industrial Revolution.

COPPER MOUNTAINS

The copper used on British ships came from a newly discovered mine in north Wales. However, copper hulls made the iron bolts rust away, so a new metal was needed to fix the hulls together. Copper-bottomed ships used brass, which is a mixture of copper and zinc that does not corrode.

GNOMES

The great alchemist Paracelsus believed that little people lived underground who could walk through solid rock. He called them gnomes. Miners believed that accidents underground were caused by these gnomes, who were angry at being disturbed.

NEW FUEL

Darby's ironworks used a new source of fuel. He roasted coal to make it into coke, which burned very hot and did not add impurities to the iron. Coke is still used in modern smelters, known as blast furnaces.

METALWORKS

Zinc ore was mined in Somerset, England, and brass was made in factories called brass mills in Bristol. Abraham Darby set up the first brass mill there, but later moved to Shropshire, where he built a new kind of efficient ironworks.

BLOCK MILLS

As well as copper, the Royal Navy needed a lot of pulley blocks, a wheel device used for raising sails. Just one ship used 1,000 blocks. In 1798, a factory called the Portsmouth Block Mills was set up. It used metal cutting machines that could make blocks ten times faster than by hand.

WHAT'S NEXT?

The Portsmouth Block Mills was one of the first factories of the Industrial Revolution. Not only did it manufacture things quickly, but it was also powered in a new way—by steam engines.

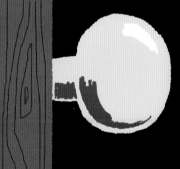

GERM-FREE

Brass kills bacteria and viruses. It is often used in door handles and other things that get touched by different people, so that we do not pass on germs.

STEAM POWER

In 1698, an engineer named Thomas Savery designed "The Miner's Friend," a revolutionary machine for pumping water out of flooded mines. Savery's idea would power the world for the next few centuries.

NO MOVING PARTS

Savery's machine boiled water to make steam, which was pushed down a pipe to the mine. Then the pipe was cooled with water, and the steam turned back into water, leaving a vacuum inside. That vacuum sucked up water from the mine, and the next jet of steam pushed it up and out of the mine.

PUSHING PISTONS

In 1712, Thomas Newcomen used Savery's idea to push on pistons, making a backward and forward motion that made a wheel spin. The spinning wheel ran pumps and other machines. In 1781, James Watt's improved design made steam engines that were much more powerful.

CLAIM TO FAME

Physicists describe the action of a machine in terms of work and power. Work is a measure of how much force is applied, and power is a measure of how quickly that work is done. In honor of James Watt, power is measured in watts. One watt is the power needed to lift 100 grams up by one meter in one second.

ON THE RAILS

Rail transportation began inside mines, where heavy loads were pulled along iron tracks by ponies. Trevithick's next vehicle was a steam locomotive for hauling coal at a large ironworks.

PUFFING DEVIL

In 1801, a Cornish mining engineer named Richard Trevithick built a steam-powered road vehicle called the Puffing Devil. He used it to carry passengers up a steep hill. Within two years, Trevithick was running the first steam-powered passenger carriages through the streets of London.

CAR CRASH

Trevithick's steam car was not the first. In 1769, Frenchman Nicolas-Joseph Cugnot constructed a gun carriage powered by steam. It moved at less than walking pace, but it still went out of control on its first drive and smashed into a wall!

WHAT'S NEXT?

As the age of the motorized vehicle began, there were some transportation pioneers who looked down on these machines—because they were flying through the air!

TAKING TO THE AIR

It may come as a surprise, but people were making flying machines before the invention of cars and trains. The simplest flying machines relied on some ancient inventions: paper, silk, and gunpowder.

ANCIENT MATERIALS

The first flying machine was made out of two ancient inventions from China: paper and silk. Paper made from wood fibers was invented in China in the first century CE. Silk is made from the cocoons of moth caterpillars, called silkworms.

HOT AIR

In 18th-century France, the Montgolfier brothers built a hot-air balloon made from silk and paper. It was varnished to keep it from burning when it was filled with hot, smoky air from a fire. In 1783, they sent a sheep, a rooster, and a duck into the air to fly over the palace of Versailles!

HYDROGEN HERO

Just a few weeks after the Montgolfier balloon flight, the French scientist Jacques Charles took off in a balloon filled with hydrogen gas. For the next 150 years, hydrogen-filled airships were the largest and most successful type of flying machine in the skies.

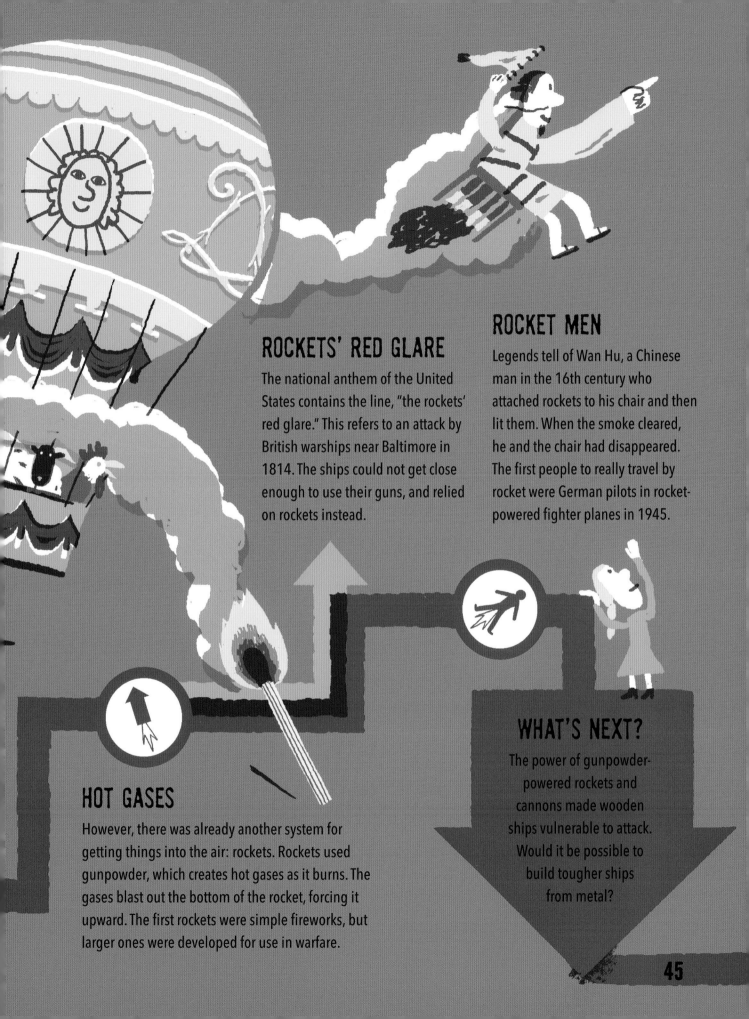

ROCKETS' RED GLARE

The national anthem of the United States contains the line, "the rockets' red glare." This refers to an attack by British warships near Baltimore in 1814. The ships could not get close enough to use their guns, and relied on rockets instead.

ROCKET MEN

Legends tell of Wan Hu, a Chinese man in the 16th century who attached rockets to his chair and then lit them. When the smoke cleared, he and the chair had disappeared. The first people to really travel by rocket were German pilots in rocket-powered fighter planes in 1945.

HOT GASES

However, there was already another system for getting things into the air: rockets. Rockets used gunpowder, which creates hot gases as it burns. The gases blast out the bottom of the rocket, forcing it upward. The first rockets were simple fireworks, but larger ones were developed for use in warfare.

WHAT'S NEXT?

The power of gunpowder-powered rockets and cannons made wooden ships vulnerable to attack. Would it be possible to build tougher ships from metal?

IRONCLADS AND STEAM LINERS

With the coming of the steam engine, ship designs began to change, making vessels faster and stronger. Two great competitions in the 19th century showed the advantages of engines and metal hulls.

STEAMING AHEAD

In 1819, an unusual ship sailed into the harbor of Liverpool, England. It was called SS *Savannah* and although it was equipped with sails, the ship also had paddlewheels powered by a steam engine. The voyage from the United States (partly under steam, partly powered by wind) had taken just 26 days.

ROAD TO RIVER

In 1804, Oliver Evans, an American inventor, built the first steam-powered amphibious vehicle. The huge vehicle's wheels fell off as it drove slowly to the river, and there are no reports of it actually afloat.

HIGH-SPEED SERVICE

Sailing ships moved faster, but they were often delayed by bad weather. A steamship would make crossings more reliable. In 1837, two rival companies launched transatlantic steamships. SS *Sirius* set off first and reached New York 18 days later—burning its furniture because it had run out of fuel! SS *Great Western* made the crossing in just 16 days—and with fuel to spare.

IRONCLADS

During the American Civil War, steamships had a different kind of clash. Each side launched an ironclad warship, which had a wooden frame armored with thick iron plates—and equipped with powerful guns. In March 1862, the two ships *Virginia* and *Monitor* fought for several hours, but neither one could defeat the other.

> GIDDYAP, TO THE EAST COAST ON THE DOUBLE!

GREAT ENGINEER

Sirius was made of wood, but *Great Western* had an entirely iron hull. Its designer, Isambard Kingdom Brunel, was involved in many advances in steam railroads, bridges, and even larger iron steamships. Along with his father, Brunel built London's Thames Tunnel in the 1830s. This tunnel was the first one to pass under a river, through soft mud. It is still used today to carry trains.

WHAT'S NEXT?

The Civil War split the United States in two. After it ended, steam-powered technology helped to put the country back together with a railroad that stretched all the way across it.

GOING LOCO

As the American Civil War drew to a close, work began on connecting the states in the east with newer territories on the west coast. A railroad would cut the journey from six months to just over a week!

TRACK TO TRACK

Two companies worked on America's first transcontinental railroad. The Union Pacific began at the Missouri River and headed west. The Central Pacific had a harder job: its workers headed east from the Pacific. They had a mountain range to cross, and their supplies had to come by ship, all the way around the tip of South America.

LOOKS LIKE THE END OF THE LINE!

STANDARD GAUGE

The distance between the rails is known as the gauge. On most railroads today, it is 4 feet 8 1/2 inches (1.4351 meters). This was set by George Stephenson as he built his early railroads. He based it on the wheels of horse-drawn wagons, which also used the rails.

RAILROAD BEGINNINGS

The first railroads were built in England by George Stephenson. In 1830, he built the first all-steam passenger railroad between Liverpool and Manchester.

RUSSIA

ARE WE THERE YET?

PYONGYANG

LONG DISTANCE

It took four years to finish the 1,800-mile (2,900-kilometer) railroad. A golden spike secured the last piece of rail where the two tracks met in Utah. At the time, this was the longest railroad in the world, but about 35 years later the Trans-Siberian railroad beat it. By 1916, this 5,772-mile (9,289–kilometer) railroad connected Moscow to the city of Vladivostok.

ALL ABOARD!

The world's longest scheduled train service uses the Trans-Siberian railroad and then changes to another track running through China to Pyongyang, North Korea. Every week, a train makes the 6,247-mile (10,214-kilometer) journey from Moscow, taking 7 days, 20 hours and 25 minutes to get there.

WHAT'S NEXT?

The steam engine powered the mightiest of machines, but smaller, more personal vehicles needed a lighter, more compact engine.

49

INNER FIRE

In a steam engine, the burning fuel is separate from the steam that pushes the moving parts. But an internal combustion engine uses the burning fuel to do the pushing—making it more powerful and efficient.

DANGEROUS FUELS

In 1807, François Isaac de Rivaz invented an engine that was powered by mixing hydrogen and oxygen—a very explosive cocktail! A (slightly) safer version was invented in 1860. This engine used coal gas, which kills you if you breathe it in. It powered the first car, the *Hippomobile*. Its top speed was less than walking pace!

HORSELESS CARRIAGE

The first practical car was made by Karl Benz in 1885. It had three wheels, ran on gasoline, and had a top speed of 10 miles (16 kilometers) per hour. In 1901, Benz's company was bought by Emil Jellinek, who named the latest models after his daughter, Mercedes. Mercedes and Benz—it has a certain ring to it!

FOUR STROKES

Most internal combustion engines use a four-stroke system. First, the piston goes up, sucking in fuel and air. When the piston goes back down, the fuel and air are squeezed. Then the fuel is ignited and the explosion pushes the piston back up. This is where all the motion comes from. When the piston goes back down again, waste gases are pushed out.

ELECTRIC CARS

Many car companies are developing high-powered electric vehicles that do not use internal combustion engines. They run on rechargeable batteries to save energy and reduce pollution.

HEAVIER THAN AIR

In 1903, Orville and Wilbur Wright built *Flyer 1*, the first flying machine with fixed wings that was heavier than the air (unlike a balloon). *Flyer 1* used a glider design but was powered by a lightweight gasoline motor.

FIRST PLANE?

Flyer 1 was the first airplane that could be steered in flight. However, in 1890 Frenchman Clément Ader had flown a steam-powered plane for 164 feet (50 meters), but it could only travel in straight lines.

WHAT'S NEXT?

Cars, trucks, trains, planes, and even some ships use internal combustion engines. However, an entirely new engine, called the turbine, would provide even more power.

DREADNOUGHTS

At the start of the 20th century, the fastest ships afloat were powered by a revolutionary new engine called the turbine. Its inventor was willing to go to great lengths to show off his engine!

UNINVITED GUEST

In 1897, the British Royal Navy held a celebration of Queen Victoria's jubilee. All the greatest ships in the fleet were lined up near Portsmouth for review by the head of the navy. Then a small—but very fast—ship zoomed into view.

CATCH ME IF YOU CAN!

IMPRESSIVE INVENTION

The ship was *Turbinia*, and it ran on a steam-powered turbine. Its inventor, Charles Parsons, was driving it to show off its power. Several naval ships gave chase, but none could catch *Turbinia*. The navy were so impressed that they added turbines to all their new battleships—making Parsons a very rich man!

SMOOTH MOTION

A turbine uses a stream of hot gas to spin a set of windmill-like blades. Unlike earlier engines, which produce a back-and-forth motion that is then used to spin a wheel, a turbine creates a spinning motion right away.

BATTLESHIPS

In 1906, the turbine-powered battleship HMS *Dreadnought* was launched. The ship's 32 guns could fire at targets 3 miles (5 kilometers) away. Enemy fire just bounced off its 12-inch (30-centimeter) steel armor! Not only that, it could sail across the Atlantic and back again with fuel to spare. After 1906, all big battleships were called dreadnoughts.

THE BATTLE OF JUTLAND

The only large battle involving dreadnoughts was the Battle of Jutland in the North Sea in 1916. A total of 250 warships from Germany and Britain fought over two days. About 8,500 people died and 25 ships were sunk.

POWER GENERATION

Today, turbines generate most of our electricity. We burn gas or coal, or use nuclear fuel, to make super-hot steam. The steam then blasts through turbines that spin around quickly, driving an electricity generator.

WHAT'S NEXT?

Dreadnoughts were seldom attacked because they were so hard to catch—and even when they came within range, they were very hard to hit. That gave inventors a new problem to solve.

HITTING THE TARGET

Until the 20th century, warships had to get within 165 feet (50 meters) to fight. A dreadnought's guns could hit a target 100 times farther away. But turbine-powered ships were fast enough to move out of the way!

RANGE-FINDING

A dreadnought had no sails, but it still had a tall mast. From up there, lookouts searched for targets. Their telescopes measured distance to the target, and within seconds of spotting a ship, the guns would fire.

STAYING LEVEL

A ship's guns move as it rises and falls with the waves. The targeting system uses a gyroscope—a spinning disk that is free to swing in all directions—to guide the guns. It stays still while the rest of the ship moves around it.

CALL IN THE COMPUTERS

However, in the time it took the shell to fly to the target, the ship would have changed position. To hit it, the lookouts needed to know the distance, direction, and speed of the target—and then calculate where it would be when the shells arrived. A person couldn't calculate it fast enough, so mechanical computers were developed to do the job.

FROM RADAR TO MICROCHIPS

Sensitive radar receivers used pure silicon crystals. Researchers found that these crystals had strange properties, which led to them being used to make the first transistors—the electronic switches in a computer microchip.

ACCIDENTAL HEATING

One day a radar researcher was testing different radio frequencies, when one particular wave melted a bar of chocolate in his pocket. We now use the same frequency to heat food in microwave ovens.

RADAR CONTROL

In World War II, ships were attacked by warplanes. A new detection system called radar showed the planes coming. It sent out a beam of radio waves, which bounced off objects and came back. The echoes of the radio waves showed where the enemies were, so ships could fire at them.

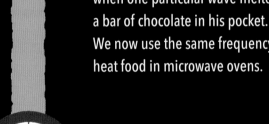

WHAT'S NEXT?

To beat radar, pilots needed speed to take the enemy by surprise—and get out of trouble fast. Once again, it was the turbine that made that possible, in a new design better known as the jet engine.

JET ENGINES

British engineer Frank Whittle invented a jet engine in 1930, but no one was willing to pay for one to be built! They couldn't see the point of a new type of engine. However, once World War II started, both sides raced to produce jet aircraft that could outfly propeller-powered fighters.

FRANK WHITTLE
1907–1996

JET-POWERED SLED

Whittle may not have been the first to develop a jet engine. Romanian inventor Henri Coanda claimed to have built a jet-powered snow sled in 1910.

SPRAY AND SPIN

A jet engine combines ideas from steam turbines and internal combustion engines. Fuel is sprayed inside and mixed with air coming in through the front. The mixture is ignited to create a jet of hot gases. The gases blast through a turbine, making it spin and drawing in more air and fuel. Finally, the jet of gases flies out the back and pushes the aircraft forward.

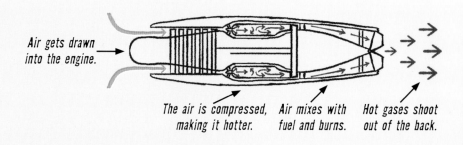

Air gets drawn into the engine.

The air is compressed, making it hotter.

Air mixes with fuel and burns.

Hot gases shoot out of the back.

TURBO POWER!

The first jet engines were a turbojet design. These are the most powerful type, and they are still used on today's fighters. Today's passenger planes use turbofan engines, which have a fan at the front to collect air and add extra thrust. They are more efficient but cannot produce as much power.

A turbofan can't break the sound barrier, but passenger jets still reach 585 miles (940 kilometers) per hour.

SPEED LIMITS

The first jet fighters were introduced by the United Kingdom and Germany in 1944. They had top speeds of 528 miles (850 kilometers) per hour—much faster than any propeller-powered rival. By the 1950s, jet aircraft were able to fly faster than the speed of sound. The fastest jet aircraft ever is the SR-71 Blackbird, which can fly at 2,193 miles (3,529 kilometers) per hour!

A BULLET WITH WINGS?

In 1947, the Bell X1 was the first aircraft to break the sound barrier. Bullets broke the sound barrier, so the X1 was designed to look like a bullet with very thin wings. However, it used a rocket engine to reach its record-breaking speed.

WHAT'S NEXT?

The jet engine's power allowed planes to go faster than ever, but that power could also be put to work in a different way—making aircraft hover!

ROTOR BLADES

Many people had dreamed of an aircraft that could fly straight up and down and hover in the air. After several failed designs, a Russian engineer called Igor Sikorsky finally cracked the problem in the 1940s.

I KNOW HOW TO SOLVE THE PROBLEM!

IGOR SIKORSKY
1889–1972

IN A WHIRL

The propeller was invented in the 1830s and was used first to power ships, then airships and finally airplanes. People wondered if a winglike propeller, or rotor, could make an aircraft fly straight up. Several designs were attempted, but they all failed. In early designs, the whirling propeller made the whole aircraft spin!

WHIRLY WING

The word *helicopter* means "spiral wing," and the rotor does the same job as an airplane wing, but in a different way. Both need fast-moving air to create the lift that pushes the aircraft up. A fixed-wing craft has to power down a runway to get the air rushing past, while a rotor can do it by just spinning around.

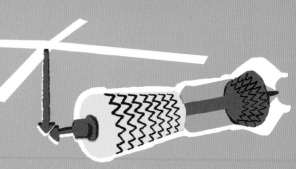

POWER SUPPLY

The first helicopters were powered by the same engines used in propeller aircraft, but helicopters needed more power to fly safely. The answer was the turboshaft, a jet engine that diverted its spinning power to the rotor.

SKY SAIL

The 15th-century Italian artist Leonardo da Vinci sketched one of the earliest helicopter designs. It had a screw-shaped sail, and although it looked as nice as da Vinci's famous paintings, it would never have gotten off the ground.

HINGE CONTROL

Sikorsky added a tail rotor to keep the aircraft from spinning. He also added hinges so that each blade in the main rotor could tilt. To make the helicopter go up, the rotors are all flat. To move forward, the hinges tilt each blade so they make more lift at the back of the rotor and less at the front—and that pushes the helicopter along.

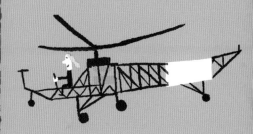

AUTOGYRO

An autogyro is half-airplane, half-helicopter. Instead of a wing it has a rotor. The rotor has no engine—the power comes from a normal propeller, but the rotor spins as the aircraft moves forward, producing lift.

WHAT'S NEXT?

Because they can land without runways and hover in mid-air, helicopters are like no other flying machine. In the 1980s, there was another revolution in aircraft: a very stealthy one.

STEALTH IN THE SKIES

By the 1980s, there were aircraft of all kinds—fast ones, large ones, small ones, ones that could fly really high or just hover. However, someone could always see them coming by using radar. Or could they?

INVISIBLE TO RADAR

Radar works because radio waves reflect off aircraft and ships, so you can see where they are. Stealth technology keeps things from being so reflective. Only a tiny part of the radar wave bounces back, so a large aircraft appears to be much smaller—something harmless, like a bird.

IT WON'T STOP WOBBLING!

WOBBLIN' GOBLIN

The first stealth plane was the F-117 Nighthawk, used by the US Air Force from 1983. It was designed with flat plates that made radar scatter in all directions—and not reflect back where it came from. It was good at confusing radar, but pilots called it the "Wobblin' Goblin" because it was difficult to steer.

SEE-THROUGH BOMBER

In 1917, the German army attempted to build a stealth aircraft: a huge bomber covered in see-through plastic. The idea was that light would shine right through the plane, making it hard to spot. Unfortunately, the wings fell off during a test flight!

FLYING WING

The next stealth plane was the B2 Spirit, an odd-looking bomber. The cockpit and engines were hidden away inside huge wings. The entire aircraft was covered in a dark coating that absorbed radar waves and spread out the heat from engines—so that it couldn't give its position away.

STEALTH SHIPS

The latest warships also use a stealth design. They have smooth, flat sides that reflect radar away from the detectors so they look like small boats, not mighty ships.

WHAT'S NEXT?

Before stealth technology, planes flew very high and very fast over dangerous areas so they could stay out of trouble. The next step was to go even higher—even flying through space!

SPY PLANE

The SR-71 Blackbird was a spy plane that took pictures over enemy territory. It also had an early form of the radar-beating coating. However, it got very hot when flying at full speed. The inside of the pilot's windshield could get hot enough to boil water!

SPY SATELLITES

The Space Race began in 1955. In public, the Soviet Union and the United States competed to put the first people into orbit. In secret, they were also learning how to spy on each other from space.

EYE IN THE SKY

The earliest spy satellites were launched in 1959. They took photographs with a powerful film camera. However, the plastic film had to come back down to Earth for the pictures to be developed and studied.

PHOTO CAPSULE

The satellites dropped film capsules into the atmosphere. Sometimes the floating capsules landed at sea. If the secret cargo was not collected within two days, it was designed to sink. Sometimes the capsules were caught in mid-air by daredevil pilots as they parachuted to the ground.

STARDUST

In 2004, a space probe called *Genesis* collected dust floating in space and returned it to Earth. The plan was to catch the capsule in mid-air, just like an old-fashioned spy film. However, the capsule's parachutes failed and the catchers missed. Oops!

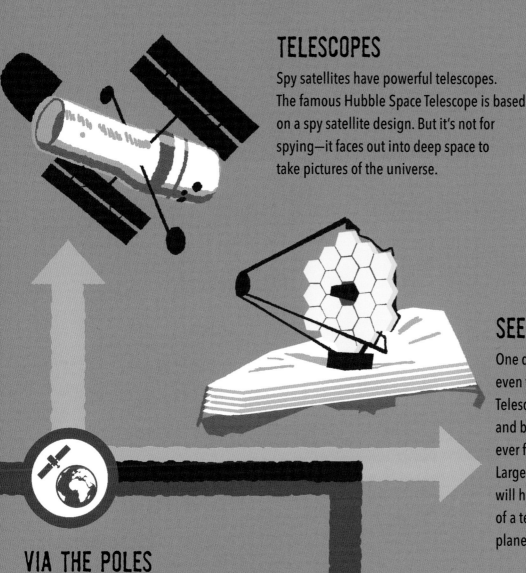

TELESCOPES

Spy satellites have powerful telescopes. The famous Hubble Space Telescope is based on a spy satellite design. But it's not for spying—it faces out into deep space to take pictures of the universe.

SEEING FARTHER

One day, new telescopes will see even farther. The James Webb Space Telescope will look for heat, not light, and be able to see the first stars that ever formed. On Earth, the Extremely Large Telescope (being built in Chile) will have a mirror three times the size of a tennis court and be able to see planets around other stars.

VIA THE POLES

By the 1980s, spy satellites used digital cameras, so pictures could now be sent back as radio signals. Many of these satellites have an orbit that passes over the North and South Poles. But they are not spying on polar bears or penguins! As they go around and around the poles, Earth slowly spins beneath them, allowing them to observe the whole planet.

WHAT'S NEXT?

Spy satellites are very secret, but there is another group of satellites that everyone can use. This is the Global Positioning System, which is yet another invention that helps us navigate.

GPS NAVIGATION

Today, navigation could not be easier. Vehicles have satnav devices (short for "satellite navigation") that tell them where they are and how to get to a destination. This system took nearly 20 years to develop and involves dozens of spacecraft.

SATELLITE CONSTELLATION

A satnav picks up signals from GPS satellites (short for "Global Positioning System"). The first GPS satellite was launched in 1978, and today there are 31. They orbit at 12,550 miles (20,200 kilometers) above Earth, and there are always at least three of them high above you, wherever you are on Earth.

WHAT'S YOUR ORBIT?

Space stations and spy satellites are in a low-Earth orbit, around 435 miles (700 kilometers) above Earth, while the ones that send out TV signals are much farther out—around 22,370 miles (36,000 kilometers). At that altitude, satellites orbit at the same speed as Earth spins, so they stay over the same part of Earth all the time.

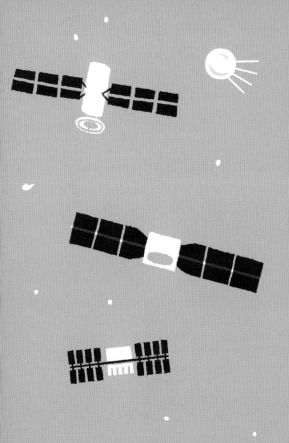

BEAMED POSITIONS

Before GPS, ships and aircraft crossing oceans used beacons spread along the coast that sent out pulses of radio waves. Each pulse would arrive at a ship or aircraft at different times—and that showed how far away each one was.

TIME DIFFERENCE

The GPS signals take time to travel to the navigation device. A message sent at 12:00 a.m. exactly might arrive a fraction of a second later. The satnav can use the time it was received to figure out how far away the satellite is. Comparing signals from three or more GPS satellites allows the satnav to calculate where it is.

I'M HERE, NOW

Each GPS satellite carries an atomic clock, which only loses a second every 100 million years or so. We can tell exactly where each satellite is, every second of every day. The satellites send out radio signals that say where they are at what time, and these signals are picked up by the satnav.

WHAT'S NEXT?

Launching any kind of satellite is an expensive business. The rockets that do it can only be used once. The space shuttle was different—it was a reusable spacecraft.

THE SPACE SHUTTLE

Most spacecraft only make one journey. If people are on board, a small return capsule brings them home. But NASA's space shuttle launched like a rocket and landed like an airplane. These vehicles were designed to go into space many times, as a satellite delivery fleet.

ENGINES ON

To get into space, the shuttle was attached to two booster rockets. These were packed with solid fuel, and once ignited, the rockets could not be turned off. In other words, the boosters were immense fireworks.

FROM COLD TO HOT

The shuttle also had three of its own rocket engines, powered by liquid hydrogen and liquid oxygen. The spacecraft carried the fuel in a separate tank, which fell off once the shuttle reached space. Parts of the fuel tank had to be kept at −418 °F (−250 °C) to keep the fuel liquid. But when the fuels were mixed they burned at 5,970 °F (3,300 °C)—almost as hot as the Sun!

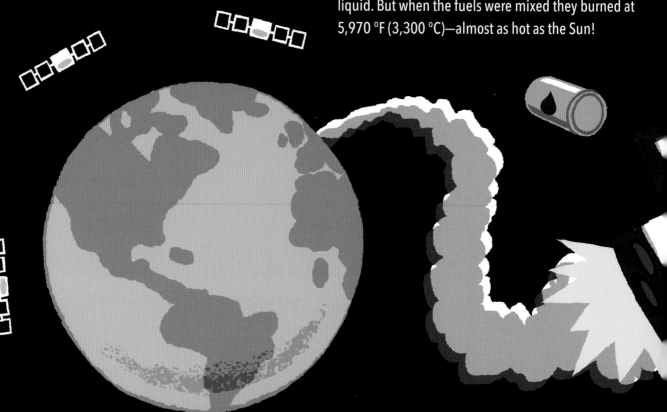

CALENDAR PROBLEM

The space shuttle was the most advanced spacecraft ever made, but on early missions it could not fly over New Year. The computer clock on board could not go from December 31 to January 1!

UP IN ORBIT

The shuttle orbited about 220 miles (354 kilometers) above Earth. It was positioned upside down, with its tail and cabin facing Earth. In between was a cargo bay. Its robot arm was used to haul satellites out of the bay and launch them into space. The arm could also grab old satellites and bring them home.

HEADING HOME

The shuttle's engines were no use on the flight home, making it the world's largest, heaviest, and fastest glider. The pilot slowed down by zig-zagging through the air and then landed at 220 miles (354 kilometers) an hour! That is much faster than a regular plane, so the shuttle needed a runway twice as long as normal.

WHAT'S NEXT?

NASA's shuttle fleet flew 135 missions between 1981 and 2011. The space shuttle was the first of its kind, and building it required new space-age materials.

TOUGH TILES

NASA's space shuttle designers needed materials that were lightweight, strong, and wouldn't be damaged by extreme temperature. In the end, they used the stuff in sand and soot!

DIFFICULT MISSION

In space, it is sometimes very cold and sometimes very hot, and as the spacecraft heads home, it becomes an artificial shooting star—with people inside! The space shuttle had to be tough enough to do this over and over again.

FRICTION

A spacecraft gets hot because of the friction, or rubbing force, of the air rushing past. Count Rumford showed how friction made heat back in the 1790s. He started drilling a hole in a cannonball placed in a barrel of water. The motion of the drill was converted into heat—and eventually the water began to boil!

DOUBLE-CARBON

The shuttle's nose cone and wing edges were a more high-tech version of soot, the pure carbon left behind by fire. Sheets of carbon fibers were molded into shape and baked hard. Then the gaps were filled with chemicals that transformed into pure carbon and glued the sheets together. They were an example of composite materials, where several different substances are made to work together.

Tiny strands of carbon— as thin as spider's silk but stronger than steel— can be woven into fabric.

THE FIRST COMPOSITE MATERIAL

The first composite material was not that high-tech. Mud bricks are a mixture of water, earth, and straw— and perhaps animal poop, too. People have been building with them for 9,000 years.

HEAT SHIELD

The top of the shuttle was covered in white tiles made of silica, the same material as in grains of sand. The tiles reflected heat away and kept the shuttle from getting too hot in bright sunlight. The underside was covered in black silica tiles. The black came from dark glass made with boron, which could withstand the 2,300 °F (1,260 °C) fireball that forms around the spacecraft as it enters the atmosphere.

WHAT'S NEXT?

The technology used in the space shuttle has been applied to many other things. Today's aircraft are also built from composite materials, making them lighter, larger, and less polluting.

SUPER-JUMBO VEHICLES

In the 21st century, passenger aircraft are making use of composite materials. There are plans for future composite aircraft which will change long-distance travel in amazing ways.

LARGER AND LIGHTER

The first modern airliners took to the air in the 1950s. They were made almost completely of metal, which made them heavy. A full tank of fuel could take 200 passengers across the Atlantic Ocean. Now, more than half of each high-tech airliner is made from lightweight composites. These planes can hold 500 passengers, and fly halfway around the world.

KEROSENE

Jet engines do not use the same fuel as cars. Instead of gasoline, they use kerosene, which is much thicker and harder to burn. But when it is ignited it releases more heat.

SMART STRUCTURE

The strongest sections of the modern aircraft are still metal. They are made from a mixture of aluminum and titanium, which is light but also very strong. The wings and body are made from carbon fiber. Strands of pure carbon are woven into sheets that can be glued together and baked hard.

LONG-DISTANCE

The first private spacecraft was launched in 2004. SpaceShipOne was built of composite materials. It was carried high into the sky by an aircraft, and then dropped in mid-air. The rocket engine then blasted the craft into space before it flew down again and landed like a plane. Space tourists may use this kind of craft in the future.

BIGGER OR FARTHER?

The two main composite airliners are the Airbus A380, known as the SuperJumbo, and the Boeing 787, or Dreamliner. The A380 is a double-decker plane with room for more than 500 people. It flies between the world's biggest cities. The Dreamliner is smaller but can fly farther without having to refuel.

A BETTER VIEW

By 2050, Airbus are planning aircraft with see-through walls, which will give passengers a better view as they fly. Don't look down!

WHAT'S NEXT?

Advances in technology continue to change transportation. Soon, we will all have vehicles that drive themselves. In fact, there is a spacecraft that can do that already.

SPY ROCKETS

A drone is an aircraft that has no crew onboard and is controlled from the ground. The word *drone* can apply to anything from a toy to a warplane. Perhaps the ultimate drone is the X–37B: a rocket–powered robot spaceplane that can stay in orbit for months.

SECRET MISSION

The X-37B is a top-secret spacecraft used by the US Air Force, first launched in 2010. They have not told anyone what it is for. It may be testing secret space weapons, or it may be spying on other countries or spacecraft. Some people think it can carry space commandos on secret missions. No one knows!

SHHHHH!

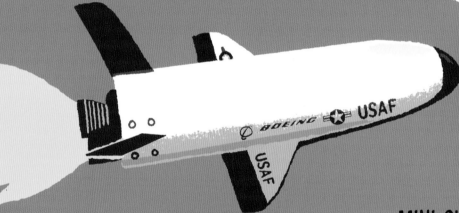

BOEING ★ USAF

USAF

I WONDER WHAT THEY'RE DOING?

MINI SHUTTLE

The X-37B looks a little like a space shuttle (see pages 66–69), only much smaller. The shuttle was half the size of a jumbo jet, while the X-37B is only a little longer than a bus. The X-37B is launched on top of a rocket. It uses wings and the same heat-proof tiling system as the shuttle for gliding back home.

LONG TIME, NO SEE

The only thing we really know about the X-37B is that it stays in space for a long time. It has solar panels on its cargo hold to make the electricity it needs while in orbit. The longest mission so far has been 675 days—that's nearly two years! There may be an X-37B up there right now…

> I HOPE I DIDN'T LEAVE THE IRON ON!

LIVING IN SPACE

In March 1995, Valery Polyakov returned from a stay in space aboard the *Mir* space station. He had been there since January 1994, earning him a record stay in space of 437 days.

MICRODRONE

Because drones don't need to carry a crew, they can be very small. The smallest drone is the Black Hornet. It is only 4 inches (10 centimeters) long and can fly at 11 miles (18 kilometers) per hour for 90 minutes, sending back video at the same time.

WHAT'S NEXT?

Sending drones into space is much easier than sending people into orbit. However, if engineers can find a material strong enough, one day we might just take an elevator.

AN ELEVATOR TO SPACE

Imagine if all you needed to do to go into space was to step into an elevator! A space elevator sounds crazy, but it could be the least expensive system for getting into orbit.

EUREKA!

KONSTANTIN TSIOLKOVSKY
1857–1935

AN OLD IDEA

A Russian math teacher named Konstantin Tsiolkovsky had the idea for a space elevator in 1895. He also figured out the amount of rocket power and speed needed to get into orbit, and described future space technology such as booster rockets and space stations.

HOW IT WORKS

A space elevator would need to be 45,000 miles (72,420 kilometers) high—nearly six times the width of Earth. At the top would be a counterweight, which would orbit at the same speed as Earth turns. It would keep the cable straight and always pointing straight up. Travelers and cargo would be winched up and down the cable.

SPACE WALKER

In 1984, Bruce McCandless became the first spacewalker to travel through space unattached to his spacecraft. He used a rocket pack to fly around the space shuttle.

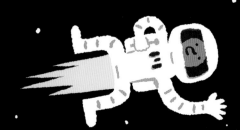

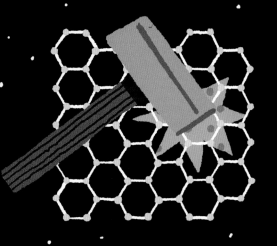

CARBON SHEETS

Graphene might be strong enough to make a space elevator. This amazing material is made from sheets of carbon that are one atom thick. If they are rolled up and woven together, they could make material much stronger than steel, but a fraction of the weight.

UP AND DOWN

Although traveling up the space elevator could be slow, it would be very efficient. On the way down, the elevator would be pulled by gravity, and as it fell, that energy could be used to generate power for the next upward journey.

TALL TOWER

The largest building being made at the moment is the Jeddah Tower in Saudi Arabia. It will be the first structure that is more than 1 kilometer (0.6 miles) tall. That would leave only 72,419 more kilometers to go!

WHAT'S NEXT?

There are no plans to build a space elevator. Who knows if it is even possible? But 8,000 years ago, no one knew they could make metal engines, use stones to navigate, or make spacecraft. It's time to find the next link.

TIMELINE

Here is a reminder of all the links that we've followed so far. Do you think that you might figure out the next link in the chain?

Beginning of time: Volcanic eruption!

A volcano spews out hot lava that cools into solid rocks. Rocks contain all kinds of natural minerals, including pure sulfur and other colorful chemicals.

35,000 years ago: The first paintings

Early humans use powdered rocks and ash to decorate caves. They make paintings of ancient animals, spirits, and even self-portraits.

1783: Taking to the air

While inventors struggle to improve transportation by land and water, the Montgolfier brothers in France invent a whole new way of traveling with the hot-air balloon.

1700s: The birth of steam

Ships were the first mass-produced vehicles, and the factories used a new source of power—the steam engine. Before long, steam engines were powering the ships as well.

1860: The internal combustion engine

Transportation is revolutionized by the invention of the internal combustion engine. Soon these engines are driving cars, trains, boats and even the first airplanes.

1944: The first space rocket

A rocket-powered bomb designed in Germany becomes the first vehicle to enter space. Within 25 years, rockets are launching satellites and sending humans to explore the Moon.

1981: The first reusable spacecraft

The space shuttle first flies, taking off like a rocket and landing like a plane. To protect it, engineers use chemicals made from common rocks— just like ancient inventors.

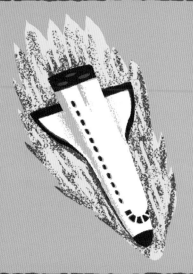

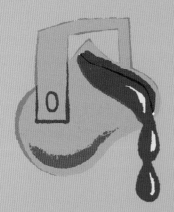

8,000 years ago: Smelting bronze

Minerals burn in hot fires and release metals that are mixed to make a strong material called bronze. Bronze technology leads to the rise of great civilizations.

3500 BCE: Inventing the wheel

Bronze Age civilizations invent the wheel and use it to make pottery, as well as road vehicles and war chariots.

1200 CE: Using magnets to navigate

Iron technology includes magnets, and magnetic compasses become a very important tool for navigation. Explorers can travel much farther without getting lost.

1200 BCE: Iron replaces bronze

Bronze becomes scarce and is replaced by a harder, tougher metal: iron. Iron Age civilizations take over from Bronze Age ones.

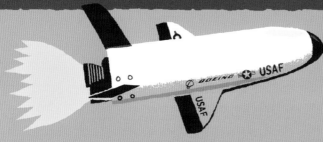

2015: The longest flight?

A rocket-powered space drone called the X-37B, which flies in space by remote control, launches for a secret mission expected to last two years.

PRESENT DAY: WHAT'S NEXT?

We now have satnavs, space rockets, and stealthy spy planes. The technology used to develop these could be applied to even more amazing inventions. Where will technology take us next?

GLOSSARY

alloy a mixture of two or more metals that blend together to make a single metallic substance

amphibious able to function in water and on land

atmosphere the blanket of gases around a planet or moon

axle the rod that connects two wheels. A wheel turns around the axle at its center.

bacteria tiny living things that have a body made of a single cell

carbon a chemical element that exists in different forms, including diamond and soot

chariot a two-wheeled horse-drawn cart where the riders stand up

compass a magnetic navigation device that always points north

composite materials materials made of two or more substances that are bonded or woven together to create a single material with special properties

crystal a solid in which the atoms are arranged in an orderly pattern

drone a flying machine with no crew on board, operated by remote control

eclipse an event in which the Moon or Sun is temporarily blocked from view

equator an imaginary line around the middle of Earth, splitting it into two halves called hemispheres

friction the force that makes substances rub against each other instead of sliding past one another smoothly

fulcrum the turning point of a lever. A fulcrum can also be called a pivot.

Global Positioning System a system of satellites that communicate with navigation devices to calculate exact locations on the surface of Earth

gyroscope a device for detecting the motion of a vehicle. The gyroscope always stays still while the vehicle moves.

horizon the line at which Earth's surface and the sky appear to meet

hull the main body of a ship, including the bottom and sides

hydrogen a lightweight gas that is very easily ignited

kiln a hot oven for baking pottery or bricks

knapping knocking flakes off a rock. Stone tools are made by knapping.

latitude a measure of how far north or south you are on Earth's surface

lodestone a natural magnet made of iron-rich rock

longitude a measure of how far east or west you are on Earth's surface

mass production the process by which a product is made in large amounts

meteor a space rock that enters Earth's atmosphere and burns to form a shooting star

meteorite a meteor that hits the surface of Earth

minerals naturally occurring solids that make up rocks

navigate to find your way from a starting point to a destination

obsidian a dark glass mineral formed by cooling lava

orbit the path that a smaller object follows around a large one, such as Earth's path around the Sun

ore a mineral that contains large amounts of a useful substance, such as a metal

piston a rod that sits inside a cylinder and moves up and down

potter someone who makes pots or other objects from clay

pulley a machine made up of a rope running around one or more wheels, used for lifting weights

pumice a light, porous stone formed when air bubbles get stuck inside cooling lava

radar a machine that detects distant objects by bouncing radio waves off them

react when one substance combines with another to make a completely new substance

rocket a type of engine that is powered by burning gases

rotor a rotating wing

rudder a flat device that can be moved back and forth to steer a vehicle, such as a ship

satellite an object that orbits another larger object in space

sextant an instrument for measuring the height of the Sun, Moon, or stars above the horizon

smelting the process that separates a pure metal from its ore

sound barrier the conditions that an aircraft must break through to travel faster than the speed of sound

steel an alloy made mainly of iron and carbon

suspension a system that suspends a vehicle over its wheels to give a smoother ride

tsunami a giant wave caused by an undersea earthquake or other catastrophe

turbine a machine that spins around when gas or liquid flows through it

vacuum a space with nothing inside, not even air

volcano an opening in Earth's crust from which hot, liquid rocks can escape from underground

INDEX

aircraft 45, 51, 56–61, 69, 70–71, 72–73
airships 44
autogyros 59

bone china 19
brass 40, 41
Bronze Age 16–19, 20, 22

calculator 8
cars 50–51
carts 20, 21
cave paintings 8–9
charcoal 9
chariots 21
clocks 36, 37, 65, 67
coaches 21
coke 41
Columbus, Christopher 30–31
compasses 24, 25, 26–27, 32
composite materials 69, 70
copper 13, 15, 16, 39, 40

dead reckoning 32–33
dreadnoughts 53, 54
drones 72–73
dyes 38

Easter Island 11
electric cars 51

feng shui 25
flint tools 11
friction 68
fulcrums 19

glass 10, 15
gold 13
GPS navigation 64–65
graphene 75
gunpowder 7, 45
gyroscopes 54

helicopters 58–59
Henry the Navigator 28–29
horsepower 21
hot-air balloons 44

internal combustion engines 50, 51
iron 22–23, 24, 25, 26, 47

jet engines 56–57, 58, 70

knapping 11
knots 32

latitude 34–35
lava 10
lead 12, 13, 14, 39
levers 19
lodestones 24, 25, 27
longitude 36–37

machines 18–19, 42
magnets 24, 27
Mars 25
metals 12–15, 16, 22–23, 26, 39, 40, 41, 47, 70
meteorites 13
microwaves 55
Minoans 16, 17

navigation 24, 26–27, 32–35, 37, 64–65

obsidian 10, 11

paints 9, 24
potter's wheel 18, 20
propellers 58
pulleys 18, 41
pumice 10

radar 55, 60, 61
rail transportation 43, 48–49
ramps 18
rockets 45, 65, 66, 71, 72, 74
rollers 20
rotors 58–59

satellites 62–65, 67
sextants 34, 35, 37
ships 28–29, 38–41, 45, 46–47, 52–54, 61
shipworms 38, 39

silica 69
smelting 12, 13, 15, 22, 41
space elevator 74–75
space shuttles 66–69
spaceplanes 4, 71, 72–73
spy satellites 62–63
stealth technology 60–61
steam power 42–43, 46–47, 50, 51, 52
steel 23
Stone Age 8, 11
sulfur 6–7, 39
sundials 34

telescopes 33, 54, 63
time zones 36, 37
tin 14, 22, 23
transistors 55
Trojan War 17
turbines 52–53, 55, 56

volcanoes 6, 7, 10

watts 42
wedges 19
wheels 18, 20, 21, 42
wind directions 33